Builders' Blunders

By Barry Matthews

Copyright © 2017 'Barry Matthews'

All rights reserved.

ISBN: 1535273313
ISBN-13: 978-1535273312

CONTENTS

Introduction	4
De Ice-Ice, Baby	7
You Only Comply Twice	11
The Great Bottomless Concrete Pit	15
Hang In There, Steel-Fixers!	18
Out Of The Darkness…	23
Silence	27
Hammer To Fall	31
If The Mask Fits…	36
Do Not Crush The Boss's Car!	40
Search For The Lost Tower Crane Bases	44
Mixer Mix-Up	48
Sleeping On The Job	52
Sacked From The Sky!	56
The Carpetbaggers	61
Ducting For Cover	65
Hell Hath No Fury…	69
Mind The Meat And Two!	73
Le Tour De Site	77
Anyone For Ice Cream?	81
Feeling A Bit Flat…	85
The Tale Of Blondie Bill	89
Postscript	93

INTRODUCTION

My name is Barry Matthews. Well it isn't. I've published this book under an assumed name for reasons that I think are obvious.

On and off for the last four decades, I've worked on building sites across the south-east of England, the Midlands and London. These have ranged from major civil engineering projects worth billions of pounds to tiny renovations costing a few thousands. I've worked on the tools doing the really nasty shifts, and I've worked as a foreman making other people do it for me. I've worked with more materials, more tools and more nationalities of builder than you could possibly dream of. So it's fair to say I know the construction game pretty well by now.

You can probably guess how the idea for this book came about. I was sat in the pub one day with my son Antony (not his real name, either) and I told him one of the many mad things I've seen on site over the years. Then he came out with the immortal line:

"I bet you've got enough to write a book."

So I have. It's not an especially long or detailed

book, and I've not written it to make money. I just wanted to get these stories down in print, have something to look back on with a smile in my retirement, and hopefully give you a good laugh in the same way these adventures do for Antony and the other regulars down at my local. Of course, if you work or have worked in the construction industry, I'm sure you'll recognise plenty of the goings-on in here as normal everyday stuff…

Everything I've put in this book is true to the best of my recollection, although I'm sure you'll understand why I've had to be pretty general and vague when it comes to descriptions of the sites I was working on, the work I was doing and the people I was working with. There's plenty of stuff I'd have loved to have told you, but couldn't for fear of ending up in the dock.

Making and fixing things is my skill in life. Writing is not. Thankfully, my son is the complete opposite. He's carved out a successful writing career for himself but couldn't even repair a puncture on his bike unaided until he was 28. He has kindly taken my stories and put them into print for me, and didn't even mind when I insisted keeping some of the fruitier bits of swearing in - no easy task for a soft tosser like him. In all seriousness, though, I'm really grateful to him for putting this together and just as glad that he hasn't made me look like a prize twat (as far as I can see).

From my experience, stories like this are best enjoyed over a beer. So get a pint in, sit back, relax and shake your head in disbelief at the things you never thought could happen behind the signs that say: 'Hard Hats Must Be Worn Beyond This Point'.

DE-ICE ICE, BABY

Building company bosses hate having workers sat around doing nothing when the weather is crap and there's nothing you can do about it. They sit there, peering out of their site offices at the pouring rain and what do they see? Everyone huddled around in a shelter on the other side of the site, smoking roll-ups, drinking tea, ogling the tits on page three (back in the old days) and getting paid for it.

It's even worse when everything looks seemingly fine but there's an unforeseen and (supposedly) fixable issue to get people working. Like ice, for example. Unfortunately, these issues tend to be resolved by using a sledgehammer to crack a walnut, as was the case in this story from one of the biggest jobs I've ever worked on. And it was an expensive, ineffective and polluting sledgehammer at that.

It all happened during an especially cold snap during what was already a nasty winter, on a job that required huge expanses of concrete floors and walls to be built. We'd done most of the flooring, but would come onto site at 7:00 each morning to find big patches of ice on top of the concrete we'd laid. Obviously, it would have been incredibly dangerous to have set to work sliding around like Bambi on a frozen pond, so we had to sit there and wait for the winter sunshine to thaw it off. It was normally about 8:30 by the time we could get going.

Of course, management didn't like this 90 minutes of paid time-wasting every morning, not to mention the delays it could cause to what was one of the biggest engineering projects in the country at the time. So some bright spark decided to try blitzing the ice with some de-icer.

We're not talking a few of the spray cans out of Halfords here. Truckloads of aviation-grade de-icer were brought in from God knows where and at enormous expense. If you've ever boarded a plane and been sat waiting to leave while a giant wand sprays from window to window, you'll know the kind of stuff I'm talking about.

So in came this truck: the concrete got hosed down, the ice thawed in minutes, was washed away into natural drainage and then we were allowed to get cracking. All good so far.

What the dickheads in management didn't know was that the de-icer they were using contained a number of chemicals that were very harmful to the environment. They simply had no idea that when it's used in airports, this de-icer runs off into localised drainage tanks, where other solutions are added to it to neutralise harmful effects to animals and wildlife. Then, once these solutions had done their stuff, the waste was released into regular drainage, be it man-made through pipes or natural run-off like rainwater.

I can only imagine what their faces looked like

when the environmental complaints started coming in. These stated that the local streams around the site were experiencing unusually high levels of pollution due to these de-icer chemicals. But rather than abandon the whole thing and let nature take its course with the ice the next morning, they were dead-set against giving up, presumably because they didn't want to make themselves look like complete twats.

So out came the chequebook once again and in came some drainage tanks so that this de-icer could be treated on-site before being released. By this stage, however, the whole thing had become much more complicated and specialised. So much so that trained staff with the necessary qualifications were now needed to conduct the whole thing safely and legally.

Off went a few of the more senior blue-collar lads onto the requisite courses – at further cost to the management – so that they could come back and do it. Which they did, and for a little while everything (apart from the outgoings from the corporate bank account) was fine, with the whole process falling into place every time there was a decent overnight frost.

The only problem was that those trained-up blokes then suddenly cottoned on that if they were qualified to operate the de-icing mechanisms on a building site, then that they'd be qualified to do the same job at an airport. And once they realised that they'd get more money working in a better environment at the major international airport up the road, and that said airport was looking for extra staff to keep them running through the cold snap, they were off quicker than you could say 'cabin crew, seats for departure'.

So management had invested Christ knows how many thousands of pounds into the de-icing equipment and the gear to treat it, but suddenly found it unusable because they had no-one with the required tickets any more. So what did they do? Yup, you guessed it – find another bunch of willing bods and send them off on the same course! Inevitably, this cycle repeated itself another couple of times, only eventually halted by the warmer weather of spring.

To be honest with you, in the world of construction, incidents like these are par for the course. They normally follow this simple three-step procedure:

- management introduce new idea to save time, or more importantly, money
- idea doesn't work and it turns into an almighty balls-up
- management burn through as much cash as is necessary to rectify the problem without going back to how things were in the sodding first place.

Of course, these managers carry on, either wilfully in denial or blissfully unaware that it would have been far cheaper to pay the blokes for the time they were iced off, rather than splurge the cash on high-grade de-icer, the equipment and solutions to clean it, and several places on a course to qualify people in using it.

Then again, in hindsight I suppose there was one upside. Britain's airports have probably never had so many qualified de-icing staff to choose from.

Chocks away!

YOU ONLY COMPLY TWICE

This is a story of miscommunication taken to the next level, combined with a workforce with a sense of humour wicked enough to let their boss stitch himself up monumentally.

I was part of a team putting up concrete walls on a big civils job in east London. Those of us on the tools got along well enough, but as is so often the case, we found the general foreman to be a bit of a pain in the arse most of the time. His deputy, on the other hand, seemed far more switched on and good at dealing with the 'ground troops', so to speak.

One Monday morning, a clerk had come round to inspect our work, and found that some of the walls didn't quite meet the specification laid out in the brief. The errors weren't major, like putting it in the wrong place on site (has happened before) or leaving a hammer inside the shutter when the concrete was poured (has also happened before!). But if the brief says the walls have to be perfect to the millimetre, then perfect to the millimetre they must be.

So the clerk duly filled out a non-compliance

report (NCR), detailing the mistakes that he'd spotted. This is then normally passed to the general foreman, who makes the decisions on how the mistakes are to be rectified, whether that be making small adjustments here or there, or ripping everything up and starting again from scratch.

On this particular Monday morning, however, the general foreman on this job was away on the first day of a two-day course. So it was left to his deputy to read the report and realise that there was no way of solving the problem while keeping the existing poured concrete. He duly ordered us to break up the entire wall and start over.

It was a bit of a pain for us having to do the work, but at the end of the day, these things happen and we were still getting paid. So down came the old wall, off went the old concrete to be broken up and disposed of, and up went the new wall the following day, this time meeting the specification exactly.

The deputy general foreman seemed happy enough and all was well. But what we didn't know at that time was that no paperwork was then filed to confirm that the new wall had been completed and that the non-compliance report had now been, well, complied with.

Come the next (Wednesday) morning, the general foreman returned from his two-day course and got back to his usual duties. Ideally, he'd have had a chat with his deputy to catch up with the goings-on from the previous days, but that wasn't possible... because the deputy had gone off on the same two-day course.

Instead, the foreman had to resort to all the paperwork that was left in his in-tray in the site office. There he found an NCR from Monday saying that a wall that had been constructed did not meet the required specification. And that NCR wasn't accompanied by any documentation to say the required changes had been completed.

Now, as I said at the start of this story, this general foreman wasn't easy to deal with. Especially when he thinks that some of his workers have been dicking about for two days in his absence without them acting on an NCR. So out of the site office he comes, stomping towards us, shouting and raving his head off with something along the lines of:

"Why the fuck haven't you got this fucking wall done? It's been two fucking days since the NCR was done and you've done fuck all about it. Get that new wall built NOW!"

When a foreman goes off like a volcano, trying to reason with him is futile, even to explain something as simple as the new wall already being in place. There was no paperwork to say that the new wall had been constructed (and those of you who have worked in the industry will know that paperwork is *everything*). The only Plan B would have been to get the deputy in to back us up and explain the situation, but he was off on his course. So we had no way of getting this foaming-at-the-mouth general foreman down off his high horse.

This left us with only one course of action: tear down the new wall, send that concrete off to be broken up and build a wall on that same spot for the third time that week. It was a ridiculous state of affairs, but no-one was going to kick up a fuss about something that basically gave them two days' extra work and pay.

Fast-forward to Friday morning and the deputy

general foreman is back on site, and finally has a chat with his superior. Both mentioned to each other that the issues mentioned in the NCR had been rectified and that it could be neatly filed away as 'completed'. Neither knew that those issues had in fact been rectified twice over.

Rather than front up and tell the pair of them about the error, we decided between us that it would be funnier for us, and more embarrassing for the general foreman, to see how long it took before they found out through other means. Given the amount of mixed concrete that went to our part of the site over the course of that week, and the amount of broken concrete that came out of it, we all figured someone elsewhere would spill the beans at some point.

Unfortunately, by the time I left the job a few weeks later, neither of them were any the wiser. I wonder if they ever found out?

THE GREAT BOTTOMLESS CONCRETE PIT

I'm sure from the title alone that you've already got a pretty good idea of where this story is going. Well, if you take the seriousness of how bad you think this is going to be, and multiply that by about three, then you might be able to grasp the severity of the situation.

This happened a long time ago, in the relatively early days of my career. I was working on the renovation of a big retail store, slap bang in the middle of a busy high street in a large town up north. As part of this revamp, we had to build up some shutters (temporary wooden structures into which concrete can be poured and left to set) in order to create a new wall in the basement. As this was a big shop, it was a big wall to match, and so we knew that a fair amount of the grey stuff was going to be needed to be pumped in from above.

The shutters were put together without any problems and the concrete mixer arrived for the pour, carrying with it around 40 cubic metres of concrete.

In went the load – and to our bemusement up at ground level, it didn't completely fill up the shutter. So in came another concrete wagon shortly afterwards with another 40 cubic metres, which was bunged straight in. Still it didn't seem like it was anything like full. In went a third load, but the top of the shutter still couldn't be reached.

Everyone was left stood around scratching their heads as to what was going on, and we were all discussing what to do in the site office. There was one question on everybody's lips: 'That isn't a 120 cubic-metre shutter, surely?'

Then the phone rang. It was the manager of the department store next door, asking in a polite but slightly worried tone whether the grey liquid that was running into the floor of his shop at an alarming rate was anything to do with us…

As quickly as we could, we darted around to take a look. What we discovered was total carnage. The concrete was pouring through into the shop, ruining rack after rack of expensive goods and coating hundreds of square feet of shop floor in soggy cement.

It didn't take long for us to work out what had happened. The wall we were pouring was on the edge of 'our' premises, adjoining a brick wall that separated the shop from the department store. Everyone was led to believe that the brick wall was 18 centimetres thick and therefore would easily hold the weight of the tonnes of concrete being poured to sit against it. But as it transpired, that brick wall just 4.5 centimetres across - just one brick deep. Why it was that way, I have no idea, but it was therefore no surprise that the brick wall soon gave way to 40 cubic metres of mushy un-set concrete - and the other 80 sent in after it.

As I was relatively junior at the time, I wasn't party to how everything was put right afterwards. I wish I had been, as the list of things that would have been taken into consideration must have been as long as your arm: breaking up and removing the excess concrete, rebuilding the brick wall (presumably to the right thickness this time), delays to the shop renovation, damage to the goods in the department store, the inconvenience and hampering trade it would have caused the department store… and Christ knows what else. Can you imagine how much that one wall giving way would have cost?

Looking back, it's quite scary to think of how much longer we could have been pumping good concrete in after bad if we hadn't been phoned. Who knows – we could have left the poor staff in the department store looking like Han Solo at the end of *The Empire Strikes Back*.

What the whole sorry affair did do, however, was teach me a valuable lesson for the future: if your shutter isn't filling up as it should and you aren't sure why, then it's probably best to stop for a bit and check the bloody thing rather than endlessly pumping in more fucking concrete.

HANG IN THERE, STEEL-FIXERS!

One thing that's certainly changed in my long time working in construction is the attitude towards health and safety.

That's not to say this isn't a good thing by any means – all the developments, standards and regulations brought in have made the industry in this country safer than it's ever been. I'm sure I'm not the only builder who's been frustrated by what we perceive as red tape, masses of paperwork and over-regulation from time to time, but without doubt the positives of this shift in culture generally outweigh the negatives. I have, at the time of writing, never sustained anything worse than a fractured ankle over my tens of thousands of hours on site, and (touch wood!) long may that continue.

It'd be extremely naïve of me, however, to claim that I don't occasionally bend the rules in order to make a difficult job a lot easier. I know I certainly have, on occasions when it's raised the risk level to myself from zero to low. Unfortunately, some people in the industry, as in any industry, are less scrupulous than others and I've seen some utterly daft and downright dangerous breaches of health and safety laws over the years. This particular one combines that complete disregard for safety, logic and common sense with a deft bit of worming out of trouble on a clever technicality.

This was a job which required a colossal amount of concrete to be poured, much of it to create imposing walls several metres high. An early part of the lengthy process of putting these walls together was the practice of steel-fixing, where reinforcing bars are put in place in a mesh-type construction around the three-dimensional area into which the concrete is going to be poured. When this is being done for a concrete floor, it's a relatively straightforward task as the fixings are laid out flat. For a big wall like this, however, it's a very different story and requires plenty of working at height.

So these two steel-fixers start from the bottom of the site of this wall and gradually work their way up, and the most efficient way for them to do that is with a scissor lift. For the uninitiated, this is a rectangular platform that can be raised and lowered as required by a metal criss-cross frame, which is controlled electrically or hydraulically so that those on the platform can work at whichever height they need to. On many sites, including this one, they're based on an electric-powered four-wheeled chassis (think very large and very slow golf buggy).

However, because all its weight is resting on wheels rather than solid or telescopic supports, there are strict limits regarding the maximum load that the platform can support. And as scissor lifts can reach several metres into the air, it's important to respect those limits as the potential consequences don't bear thinking about.

The procedure for the steel-fixers is to fit the reinforcing bars as high as they can reach, then move the scissor lift platform up a few feet to do the next bit, and keep heading upwards. This is fine in theory, but the combined weight of the fixers, their tools and the steel they were fixing put them some way over the recommended weight limit for the scissor lift. They twigged that as they got higher, it would become a real chore to have to go up and down all the time to collect the small amounts of steel they could take within the weight limit.

Keen to cut out all this faffing about, they came up with an alternative. Instead of following the laborious but correct procedure, they deliberately took on more steel than allowed, and when it came to moving up a level, they hung themselves off the steel they'd just installed and let the scissor lift ascend without them, before clambering back on and carrying on working.

I doubt that you need me to tell you that the steel fixing mesh is not in any way designed to take the weight of two grown men wearing their tool belts as well as full PPE (personal protective equipment, i.e. hard hats, boots and the like). That, combined to being suspended several floors up from the ground by their fingers, even if only for a few seconds at a time, made the whole endeavour incredibly dangerous.

By the time the safety officer on site saw what the lads were doing, they'd got quite a long way up, and the bloke went absolutely potty. Understandably so, in the circumstances. He ordered them back down to ground level and hauled them into the site office for the bollocking of a lifetime.

The lads' defence was even more astonishing than the risk they'd taken in the first place, though. While they admitted that the combined weight of men, tools and steel was well over the weight limit for the scissor lift, they pointed out that at no time was the raising or lowering mechanism operated while that limit was breached.

It was then pointed out to them that the only reason that was true was because they'd hung themselves from the steel bars they'd just fitted – in essence, preventing something dangerous from happening by doing something even more dangerous.

In response, one of the steel-fixers duly pulled out a copy of the method statement for that section of the job (the full brief of what's required and expected, including any specific safety recommendations). He plonked it on the table in front of the safety officer, and matter-of-factly said:

"Tell me where it says in there that we aren't allowed to hang ourselves from the steel."

There wasn't anything in the method statement about it, largely because it was such an insane idea that no-one would ever have thought it a realistic enough proposition to be worth mentioning in the method statement in the first place. But, in the eyes of the paperwork, they were technically correct.

Gobsmacked, the safety officer stared at them for a few brief seconds and told them to bugger off and not to do it again 'in case an accident does happen'. The steel-fixers, realising they'd managed to pull a fast one but probably wouldn't get away with it a second time, behaved themselves after that and did everything else as they should have done originally. But I don't think any action was ever taken against them, possibly because the safety officer was too embarrassed to bring up the omission from the method statement more than anything else. And as an act that dangerous on a building site would normally lead to an instant sacking, they can consider themselves bloody lucky in the end.

OUT OF THE DARKNESS…

You don't need me to tell you that construction is not a nine-to-five industry. Never has been, and almost certainly never will be. The nature of tight completion deadlines, and financial penalty clauses for building companies and contractors that don't deliver work on time, mean that unsociable hours are part and parcel of the industry.

In my time, I've done plenty of six-day weeks, seven-day weeks, 'twelve-days-on' shift patterns where you only get every other weekend off, and jobs where I've had to live away from home during the week. It can be tough, but the extra money I could earn made it worthwhile more often than not.

I've always been a fairly durable bloke when it's come to arrangements like this, but there was one particular occasion when I stretched myself a little bit too far beyond my physical and mental capabilities. And rather than it being a situation where I'd signed myself up for a job that I knew was going to be a strong, this one brought about an issue that I never would have considered in a month of Sundays.

Going back to the early years of the new millennium, I was involved in the building of a brand-new high-rise office block right in the heart of London. The building that previously stood there was demolished first, and then the new offices were constructed on a cleared site from the bottom up. And when I say 'bottom', I really mean it - a big hole was dug into the ground to construct three basement floors before we even reached surface level.

I was still on the tools back then, and I have to say that by and large, it was a shitty job down in that basement. It was dusty, it was dirty, there was little fresh air or ventilation coming in, and even though it's not normally something I suffer from, I felt pretty claustrophobic working in that kind of environment all the time.

The hours were long, too: 6:30am to 5:30pm plus a Saturday morning shift until 1:00pm, and although I was making decent money as a result, it really started to take its toll on my physical and mental well-being. But it was only after I'd been there for a few weeks that I realised that what was causing me all those issues wasn't the dirt or the claustrophobia.

I worked out that every day, I was heading down into that basement first thing in the morning, getting changed into my gear in the kit room which had been set up down there, working down there and spending all my breaks in the canteen, which had also been set up at basement level. I'd only come back up to surface level when it was time for me to scurry back to the mainline train station and travel out of London to get home.

While this doesn't necessarily sound like a problem in itself, the key was that I was on this job in the middle of winter. So when I went 'down below' at 6:30am, it was still dark… and when I resurfaced at 5:30pm, it was dark again. Or was it *still* dark? How was I to know? Having been three floors below for 11 hours straight, I had absolutely no idea whether or not the sun had actually risen that day because I never got to see it work its way across the freezing London winter sky. One day of this would feel weird to most people. But five and a half days in a row? It's enough to make a man go crazy!

The utter madness of it finally hit home at the end of one of the Saturday lunchtime shifts. The 1:00pm finish meant I had enough time to get the train back to my home town in time to make it to the football at 3:00pm (and no, I'm not going to tell you which team I support!). As it was, I'd normally be back in the pub just after 2:00pm, giving me time to have a quick pint before heading to the ground. My son Antony would always come to the football with me, and so he'd get to the pub earlier, and once I passed through the station before my stop, I'd send him a text and he'd head to the bar and get a round in just in time for my arrival. He's a good lad, looking after his old man.

Anyway, I'd got back into town, got to the pub and slumped into a chair, feeling absolutely exhausted even though it hadn't been a particularly taxing morning of work. Antony quickly spotted that I wasn't my usual self.

"Are you alright, Dad? You look done in."

"I don't feel great, to be honest, son. And I think I know why."

"What is it?"

"This is the first time I've seen sunlight since four o'clock last Sunday afternoon."

Mouth ajar, he told me to get into the gents and take a look at myself in the mirror. When I did, I didn't know who it was looking back at me. Apparently it was me - but it sure as hell didn't look like me. I looked horribly tired, with pale skin and irritated red eyes. I looked washed out, to be honest.

It was only then that I realised that I couldn't keep this up and that it was going to be seriously harmful to my health if I carried on. I don't know if it was the getting up at 4:45am every day, or a serious Vitamin D deficiency caused by the lack of sunlight, but clearly something was wrong. It might have been a different story if I was still a sprightly young man like Antony, but as a middle-aged bloke, I just didn't have it in me to keep going with it.

The next week, I started to look around for other jobs, ideally the kind that might at least have a suggestion of exposure to natural light. As it turned out, circumstance worked in my favour: the job had got to the stage where my services were required above ground level and the problem resolved itself. But ever since those literally dark days, I've always been extremely vigilant about taking jobs involving lots of underground work. I definitely don't want to go through that again!

SILENCE

Following on from my previous sunlight-free episode working on that office block development in London, there was another memorable occurrence that I can recall from that same job which took place a couple of months prior. It isn't a humorous story like the others, but one I wanted to include to show how even a hard industry like construction can surprise you with a softer side every now and again.

In the very early days of the job, it was early autumn and while we were working on the basic structure of the basement, the intermediate floors hadn't been filled in, so there was still plenty of natural light coming in. Well, as much natural light as you can imagine in the centre of London when the site is surrounded by pre-existing high-rise blocks looming overhead. But nonetheless, it was always interesting to look up and see dozens of floors of suit-clad men and well-dressed women going about their daily business, and to reflect on how completely different their working days were compared to my shifting about in the basement of a building site.

One Tuesday afternoon, work was moving along at its usual pace when, without any warning, the foreman came down ranting, raving and waving his arms around like a lunatic.

"Everyone go home! We're closed for the day! Pack up your stuff and clear off!" he cried.

No-one could really understand what was going on, and we couldn't think of any incidents or accidents that would have caused a full site closure, so I asked him what the score was.

"We've been told to close the site by the police," he said. "Someone's flown a plane into the World Trade Center in New York. They're worried there might be a similar thing in London, and with all these big office blocks around we're potentially at risk, so we need to get everyone out of the area as soon as possible." It was September 11, 2001.

Obviously, that was the first I'd heard of the terrorist attacks that were unfolding over in America that day. I gathered my gear together and made my way towards the nearest Tube station, which wasn't far away from the site, to make my way back to the mainline station and then home.

Near that Tube station was a store of one of the big electrical retailers, the kind that has loads of tellies in the window. The throng of people that had surrounded the shop window to see what was happening on the news channel being broadcast had grown to such a huge size that they were starting to block the road outside. It got so bad that the police went into the shop and ordered the store manager to turn all the tellies off because it was causing a big blockage at what, clearly, was a time where everything needed to keep moving.

While those outside the shop were initially pretty aggrieved, they eventually started to melt away in search of another source of up-to-date information. I made it onto an unsurprisingly busy Tube train and carried on my journey home, where I watched the rest of the day's events play out on the TV in my living room with my family.

I went back into work as normal the next morning, but it was clear that both on my site and in every workplace in London, a lot of people had been told to stay home. It was eerily quiet on the train, on the Tube, in the streets and on site compared to how it normally was on any other working day. But I got on with my work as best I could. And over the rest of the week, things gradually returned to normal.

But one more thing did happen that has always stayed with me. Not long after the attacks happened, all of London (well, I imagine the entire country, for that matter) came to a halt for a silence to remember those that had died. Exactly how long after 9/11 this took place escapes me, but the actual silence itself is clear as crystal in my memory.

The general foreman had told us first thing that there would be a special 15-minute break at the appropriate time so that everyone on site could safely down tools and stop what they were doing so that the silence could be properly observed. When it came to the time itself, those of us down in the basement put our tools down and got to our feet for the silence, and with nowhere else to really look around, I looked up at the sky and the office blocks above.

What I saw was hundreds - possibly even a couple of thousand - of workers in those offices, stood at the windows of their buildings, floor after floor all the way up to the top, to observe the silences for themselves. And all those workers found a central focal point - the couple of dozen builders stood way below them in a partially-constructed basement. They looked down at us and we looked up at them. When the signal came that the silence had finished, everyone went back to their normal activities, but for that brief moment, it was like being frozen in time.

In the break room later on, I was told an even more surreal story by the driver of the tower crane we had on site. After the foreman radioed up to him in his cabin, perched hundreds of feet above us, he had time to come out of his cabin and stand outside to observe the silence. He found himself in a similar situation to what we'd had in the basement, but the difference was that he was at the same height as the top floors of these office blocks. All the big bosses, with their penthouse-style offices and six-figure salaries, were looking across at this sole crane driver and he looked back.

In the complete silence of a thoughtful London, high up in the windy atmosphere, stood alone on the metal beamwork of his crane, it must have been a surreal experience for him. As it was for all of us.

HAMMER TO FALL

This is another story from an office block project in central London, albeit a different one to that which I mentioned in the previous two chapters. And while I can look back and laugh at an affair which was comic in its resolution, it's also frightening to think of what the consequences could have been. It's no exaggeration to say that those involved were very fortunate that no-one was killed.

This job was in its later stages and the building was reaching a substantial height, matching that of the other blocks immediately surrounding it. The main structure had been completed, and so it was down to guys like me working on scaffolding to do the fitting around the outside, such as insulation, windows and wall tiles.

Of all the different disciplines and hazards involved in our industry, scaffolding work can be one of the most dangerous because there are so many potential factors at play: height, the precariousness of the scaffolding itself (although that has improved massively over the years) and the tools or machinery being used. There's certainly no room for mucking about up there and it's the one place above all others where you feel pretty much permanently on guard in case something goes wrong. But, sadly, no site can be 100 per cent safe and accidents can and do happen.

I only happened to learn of this story because I was in the site office on an unrelated matter when it all kicked off. A young woman came striding into the office who clearly wasn't working on this job: she had no hard hat, no hi-vis, no boots, no other PPE, no nothing. Actually, she was a very well-dressed and quite attractive woman, but that's by the by. The four or five of us in the office fell silent as she plonked a hammer down on the foreman's desk.

"I believe this belongs to one of your workmen," she said, slightly wobbly in her voice and clearly a bit agitated.

"Oh," said the foreman, taken off guard. "Well, thanks very much for returning it to us. I'll get it back to its rightful owner. Where did you find it?"

"In my car, parked on the road just outside the gate there."

The foreman stopped for a minute to try and work out what the bloody hell was going on. Was one of his chippies (industry term for carpenters) having a bit of hanky-panky in his lunch break? Was this a wife chucking her husband out, having just found his hammer at home that morning and having smashed all his valuables to smithereens? Was she just a general nutcase? The foreman had no idea and neither did we.

After a moment, he very uncertainly ventured:

"...er, where did you find it in your car, love?"

"On the front passenger seat," she replied.

"How did it get onto the front passenger seat?"

"Through the windscreen."

There was a long pause as all our faces turned white as a sheet. That pause would have gone on forever until the woman piped up with:

"Come and have a look at my car if you don't believe me."

So out into the street we went to find that the woman was indeed telling the truth. It was obvious what had happened. Somebody working on the scaffolding on that side of the building had inadvertently dropped his hammer. Whether it was a butterfingers moment or it was just nudged by a hand or foot over the edge, we didn't know (and I still don't know now). Neither was it established just how high it had fallen. But what was clear was that the hammer had plummeted to the ground and straight through the windscreen of this poor woman's hatchback, the front seats of which were now covered in about a billion shards of glass.

Thankfully, the car was empty at the time and the woman had only discovered what had happened when she'd returned to drive away. If anyone had been sat in the passenger seat at the time the hammer hit, then, depending on how high it had fallen from, they could have suffered a broken leg at least. But in that situation, on a busy street in London on a weekday, the hammer could have landed anywhere - or on anyone – with utterly disastrous results.

I wasn't party to how the matter was resolved from the woman's point of view. I'd like to think that the construction company apologised and offered her some sort of recompense, and I'm sure she went off to make a claim through her car insurance. I know she was shaken up by it at the time but she wasn't injured physically, which is without doubt the most important thing.

What I was party to, however, was the foreman's search for the culprit. Whoever had made the mistake would have known what had happened. You don't lose a hammer without realising that it's gone, and besides, everyone on site was soon aware of the story and the commotion surrounding it.

First thing next morning, once we'd got kitted out in the changing room but before anyone was allowed to start work, the foreman summoned all the blokes on the tools into his office. He knew which guys on site could have been up on that scaffolding, and it came down to a couple of dozen of us, including myself. Straight away, with no forewarning, 'good morning' or introduction, he boomed:

"Right then, boys… HAMMERS ON THE TABLE!"

In turn, one by one, each of us walked up to his desk, took our hammers out of our tool belts and placed them down. He clearly thought that whoever had lost their hammer 'overboard' would turn up empty-handed and therefore be the man at fault. But every single man in the room had a hammer on him.

The foreman's mistake was to wait until the following morning to launch his investigation. Because that meant the culprit had the time that evening to get home and buy a replacement hammer and cover his tracks, so to speak. And so the investigation drew a blank, we all got back to work and I never heard anything else about the whole thing. Presumably the unidentified chippy got away with something that undoubtedly would have resulted in his dismissal from the job at the very least, and quite possibly further consequences beyond that.

I have to say that since then, the vast majority of sites I've worked on have mandated the use of hammer tethers when working at height. These tethers look almost identical to the flexy loop-de-loop cords you get on a landline telephone handset, with one end attached to the handle end of the hammer, and the other to the tool belt using one of those mountaineering-type screw gates. That means that now if a hammer is dropped, it simply dangles a few feet below and can quickly be recovered.

I hope I haven't made you too paranoid now. But I bet now that you've read this, you think twice the next time you walk past some scaffolding...

IF THE MASK FITS...

As I've mentioned previously, health and safety is taken far more seriously on building sites these days. The days of 'getting on with the job' are long gone, perhaps because we live in more litigious times, and there has been a huge change in culture across the industry to make sure that everyone is working as safely as they possibly can be.

To this end, workers are required to wear increasing amounts of PPE (personal protective equipment) in order to protect different parts of their body. Hard hats, glasses, steel-capped boots, gloves and hi-vis clothing are all par for the course nowadays. But one area only considered recently was the internal damage that could be caused by fumes and dust entering the lungs, and so masks that cover the nose and mouth have become commonplace too.

Originally, this meant that companies and contractors were doling out disposable masks to their workforce, but the one-size-fits-all nature of them meant that there was still the possibility of harmful material like cement dust or sawdust getting in through the small gaps between mask and face. To remedy this, the relevant workers are now required to wear bespoke fitted masks, created through what is known as a face-fit test.

How this works is that a test mask of a particular shape and size is placed over the nose and mouth of the worker. Then a hood is placed over the worker's entire head, and a test spray, which is harmless but tastes fucking horrible, is sprayed inside. If the worker can taste the fluid, then apart from wanting to be sick, they will know that the mask doesn't provide a tight seal around their face and so isn't the right size for them. This process is repeated with different sizes, and by tweaking the metal strip across the nose of adjustments, until a set-up is found that won't let any fluid reach the nose or mouth.

This is all well and good with people, like my good self, who are clean-shaven. But when blokes on site have beards, which at the time of writing are especially fashionable, it becomes impossible to fit a mask properly. In fact, even a bit of stubble can be enough to fall foul of the test. This has caused no end of problems on sites up and down the land, and created an absolute farce of a situation on one of my more recent jobs.

The section I was personally on had no problems due to the nature of the work, but the gang on the next bit along had a huge issue as the vast majority of the workforce were either beardy or stubbly. Initially this wasn't a big deal, but once it got to the stage where a lot of wood cutting and sawing was required, the issue of the face-fit tests reared its head. The general foreman, keen to make sure he wasn't caught out by any lurking health and safety officials, came over and insisted that anyone who didn't pass the face fit test couldn't do any cutting. As there were only two clean-shaven blokes on the tools, they had to do everyone else's cutting as well as their own.

Given the pain in the arse this caused to their normal workload, these two guys very quickly got cheesed off by the whole affair. There was no way anyone would let them off these duties: I could see they were annoyed, but without them, the job would have ground to a halt. But after a few days, they had finally had enough... and came back in one morning without having shaved. Their stubble meant their masks wouldn't fit to the required standard and so they, like everybody else, weren't allowed to cut.

It wasn't long until the general foreman came striding out to ask what was wrong, and discovered that no-one was clean-shaven enough to do any cutting. Clearly hacked off, the foreman picked out two other stubble-clad blokes and quietly did them a deal, offering them an extra pound an hour on their pay packets if they dropped their current workload and just did cutting all day. Happy with the offer, this new pair trotted off to the changing room, shaved straight away and within minutes had set up an impromptu cutting station, to which everyone else could take their wood to be cut to size.

For a few days, everything was fine and dandy. The cutters were happy with the extra cash, the other (bearded) chippies were happy as they got their work done without any need for hard graft like cutting, and the foreman was happy as the job was running smoothly for a change. But, as usual, all good things come to an end, and here it was caused by the cutters opening their big mouths.

Very quickly, everyone else learned that these boys were getting an extra pound an hour and wanted the money for themselves. And so the next morning, to the extreme surprise of the foreman, the whole lot of them turned up for work completely clean-shaven! As you can imagine, however, the foreman wasn't best pleased when all these other guys started demanding their extra pound 'like those two over there have got'.

Obviously, the foreman wouldn't give it to them, and as everyone was now able to do their own cutting again and there seemingly wasn't an issue any more, he deemed that everyone should be treated equally and so took the extra pound an hour away from the two cutting volunteers. Incensed by this, given the effort they'd put in to help the foreman out of a hole, the two of them told him where he could stick his circular saw (clue: somewhere painful) and walked off the job.

The foreman didn't seem too fussed by all of this as he now had a freshly shaven gang of blokes, able to wear their masks and do all their cutting. But believe me, he was extremely fussed when they all returned the following day with some freshly cultivated stubble and the whole thing started over again...

DO NOT CRUSH THE BOSS'S CAR!

It isn't difficult on a building site to spot someone important swanning about. Mainly because they aren't caked in cement, paint, dirt and seven tonnes of other crap. But on a serious note, executives and dignitaries do stand out when they come to inspect the 'ground troops' for whatever reason. It doesn't happen all that often, but most people know to make sure they're on their best behaviour for a while. One bloke I worked with in the Nineties didn't, though - and he paid a heavy price for it.

This particular chap was the driver of a machine used for breaking up wasted concrete, and he had an area in the yard which he used for doing just that, by the side of the scaffolding so he could drop concrete to be broken straight in. It wasn't specifically marked out as such, but everyone knew that it was the breaking-up area and left him to it. He was Irish and part of a sub-contractor from the Emerald Isle that had provided various bits of plant and machinery for this job, operated by one of the major London construction players.

We'd all been on the job for a few months and he'd obviously got very set in his ways in terms of the routine and procedure of breaking up the concrete and doing it in this specific area. And that was fine, until one morning when a brand-new, very shiny and very sleek luxury saloon with a personalised number plate rolled up to the main site entrance gate. It was the last kind of vehicle you'd expect to be allowed onto a site, but after a brief word with the gate man, up went the barrier and in rolled the saloon.

It pulled up slap bang in the middle of the breaking-up area, and out of the driver's door stepped an older man in sunglasses and a crisp, immaculate suit. He was trying to carry off the air of a man of true power, which he was, but in reality he was quite short and actually made himself look like a dodgy used car dealer. But I knew from previous jobs I'd worked on with the same firm that he was the big boss of this construction company.

Why he'd decided to pay our site a visit was a mystery to be. Undoubtedly it wasn't any of my business, anyway. But our machine-driving friend, completely oblivious to the signs of a VIP arriving, didn't take kindly to someone parking in *his* area. And, without wanting to revert to stereotypes about the Irish, he was typically unafraid of letting this VIP know what he thought of the choice of parking space.

"I wouldn't feckin' park there if I were you," said the machine driver within seconds of the big boss stepping from the car.

"I can park where I fucking well like," replied the boss, who was clearly irritated at the machine driver's bolshiness in addressing him like that.

"Well, don't be surprised if your feckin' motor

ends up with a big feckin' lump of concrete on it!" shouted the machine driver as he stomped off.

The boss thought better of going after him to carry on the argument. He wasn't on a social call and he clearly had important meetings with the head foremen and engineers in the site offices. So he shrugged it off, locked his car, left it where he'd parked it and headed across the yard into the office.

Ten minutes later, there was a knock on the site office door. One of the labourers poked his head in.

"What is it?" growled the boss impatiently.

"Sorry, sir, we've got a problem outside I think you need to be aware of."

"For fuck's sake. I haven't got time for shitty little problems on site. What's wrong?"

"Someone's dropped a lump of concrete onto the bonnet of your car."

I doubt there were many people on the site who didn't hear the boss's roar of "I BEG YOUR FUCKING PARDON?!", followed by the sound of the site office door being flung open and the boss sprinting over to his motor to survey the wreckage.

The labourer's description of dropping a lump of concrete onto the bonnet was the understatement of the century. A slab, probably the best part of a square metre, had been unceremoniously dumped onto the bonnet and windscreen of this beautiful car, the front half of which looked absolutely totalled as a result. It was total carnage. But before the boss had a chance to throw a full-scale tantrum about it, there was a call from the scaffolding a few floors up:

"I warned you not to feckin' park there! That's the feckin' breaking-up area!"

To this day, I'm still astonished that, in the

circumstances, the boss (just about) managed to exercise enough self-restraint not to head up the scaffolding and lamp the machine driver. But he did have his revenge. Once he found out the name of the sub-contractor the guy was working for, he went and found that subbie's most senior person on the site. The boss gave that poor team leader both barrels and told him in no uncertain terms that not only was every member of that subbie's staff immediately kicked off the job, but that the company would never consider that subbie for any work on any of its jobs ever again.

Slightly shell-shocked to have found out what happened, they all packed up their tools and headed off down the road, no doubt trying to find a way to tell their superiors in Ireland how they'd just cost their firm millions of pounds worth of contracts. I have no idea what their reaction to the machine driver would have been once they'd found out, but I doubt it was pleasant.

SEARCH FOR THE LOST TOWER CRANE BASES

If you've been reading this book through from the start, you'll have seen a pattern in the stories in that nothing that happened was ever my fault. You probably think I'm some smug git laughing at other people's idiocy and misfortune. Well, in the interests of balance, here's an example of me making myself look a complete tit on my first day in a new job.

This was another London job, but rather than putting together a building from scratch, this was a comprehensive overhaul of an existing building. It was a huge old building of eight or nine floors, with stone exterior walls, and a ground floor at street level fitted out with shops, banks and the like. All of these remained open for business while we worked turning the upper levels into modern and contemporary offices.

I came in on my first morning there, having taken up a vacancy they'd advertised for a section foreman. And after doing the normal safety induction that kicks off a first day on any site (or at least it should do!), the general foreman who was to be working above me explained that I'd been brought on board initially to oversee the erection of a couple of tower cranes and their bases. These cranes would help lift materials and other things up onto the roof for the work at the top levels, as there wasn't any practical way of getting it all up there via lift or stairs.

He told me that the cranes hadn't been put up as yet and the anchoring bases for them needed doing first. These bases are basically large boxes of concrete, easily three metres or more in height, into which the first section of the crane is encased to give it some solid stability. It's crucial work, given how vulnerable tower cranes can be to wind or other factors. Apparently, the steel-fixing for the bases was already done and was ready to have the shutters put on them so that the concrete could be poured in, so he sent me away to find them and get cracking.

Now, as this was an 'indoor' job, so to speak, there was no yard or outside space beyond the building where these cranes could be put up. What normally happens in these situations is that the cranes are based in the middle of the building, on the lowest floor, and goes through holes all the way through the roof, so that the jib and the cab on the top can be attached directly above the building.

So I made my way from the site office down to the basement level to find this steelwork, but no matter where I looked, I couldn't see anything that looked remotely like them. I asked one of the blokes working down there where they were, and he looked at me blankly and said he didn't have a clue what I was on about. I didn't want to make myself look a twat to my new boss on my first day by going back to him and saying I couldn't find them, so I spent the entire morning wandering around the whole site, hoping I might stumble upon them more or less by accident.

I managed to keep this up until lunchtime, when I was eventually rumbled by the foreman, who seemed a little dischuffed with me to say the least.

"Oi, Barry!" he said as he clocked me walking past. "It's lunchtime and you've done bugger all with those cranes so far. You taking the piss out of me, dicking around not doing any work on your first day?"

Sheepishly, I had no option to come clean.

"I'm sorry, mate. I'm not trying to be funny here, but I can't bloody find the steelwork. The guys in the basement don't know the first thing about them. I haven't got a Scooby-Doo where they are."

He chuckled at that, and seemed to be put much more at ease.

"You dozy tosser. Follow me."

With that, he took me to the main staircase and took me all the way up to the very top. He opened the fire door, led me out onto the roof and there, sat right in the middle, clear as you like, were two very well-made steel structures, ready for shuttering.

"Christ! What the bloody hell are those things doing on the roof?" I said, scratching my head.

"What, you've never seen a roof-mounted tower crane base before?" replied the foreman.

"To be honest, mate: no, I haven't. I've been doing this for a very long time, but I've never seen anything like this. I never would have thought there was anything to put the base on to support the weight of it. How the hell does this work?"

To demonstrate this, he took me back inside and back down one flight of stairs to the top floor of the building, and round the corner to where the two lifts would normally be (they'd been taken out for the duration of the job so the shafts were empty). The foreman told me to have a look upwards towards the top of the shaft, and what I saw was a bunch of RSJs, which he said were to add strength and rigidity to the shafts as the tower crane bases had been put right on top of them.

"It's the only place on the roof we could put them," the foreman said. "But I think it works pretty well, don't you think?"

I couldn't really disagree, and unusually for me, I felt like a bit of a dunce that as someone brought in as an expert, I had no concept of it even being a possibility.

Having the crane base on the roof meant that the mast was a lot shorter than it normally would have been if it had come up all the way from the basement or street level. It eventually made for a stubby little crane that could lift things into gaps and openings made in the roof.

It has to be said that the whole thing worked very well, and that while roof-mounted tower cranes are very rare, it certainly opened my eyes to a new idea in construction. I guess you're never too old to learn!

MIXER MIX-UP

There are, to an extent, good reasons why the construction industry is overrun with paperwork these days. As well as making sure people's backs are covered when something goes wrong and making it easy to find out who is liable in any given balls-up, it also helps to give clear instructions as to what is supposed to happen, and what goes where. But you can have the best-written paperwork in the world: it doesn't make a blind bit of difference if the sweaty meatbag human won't or can't read it properly.

A good example of this came on a job where I was a foreman overseeing the construction of a new road bridge. It was part of a set of improvements along this main road, including the construction of several other bridges as well as this one. As is traditional for most jobs of this nature, time schedules and deadlines were drawn up for the job which weren't in the slightest bit realistic, and so it wasn't long until we were way behind.

Whereas on a more conventional job like an office block, that wouldn't cause too much of a problem, in this case it would mean an extension to the speed reductions on this main commuter route into this particular city, causing even more misery to motorists every morning.

And then there's the thorny issue of the penalty clauses for late completion that are written in the contracts, which would quickly eat into the construction company's profit margins if the job wasn't done on time. So in order to prevent this disaster, the company introduced Saturday shifts to try and pick the pace of work up as best it could.

One Saturday morning, we were due to hold a big concrete pour to construct some columns that would act as bridge supports. We were expecting several big mixers to turn up over the course of the morning, although we weren't entirely sure how many. What we did know is that it was a big part of the job and so it would have been unrealistic to expect to get all the concrete we needed in one go.

We used the same company for all our concrete on this job, and as a result we'd got used to the same delivery drivers turning up. This was always helpful as they'd gradually got to know the ins and outs of the job, and therefore didn't need too much instruction on where to park, what to do and so on. But as this was a Saturday, all those regular drivers were off and so we had some relief drivers doing the weekend shifts. They seemed fairly clued up, though, so it didn't take long for me to explain the drill and get them pouring once they'd arrived.

Everything seemed to be going smoothly. A bit too smoothly, in fact. Over the course of that morning, more and more of these mixer lorries would turn up, do their pour, bugger off again… and then turn up again an hour later with yet another load. By lunchtime, we'd managed to do the whole pour. I couldn't believe it, and neither could the other blokes working on the site, either.

"Right then, lads, get yourself packed up," I said, happy that with a spare Saturday afternoon, I might just make it home in time for the football.

Then my mobile rang. It was my counterpart on the neighbouring bridge project on the job, about a mile and a half up the road.

"Hullo, Barry," he said. "Just wanted to pick your brains about something."

"Go ahead, mate," I replied.

"Have you had any concrete this morning?"

"Yeah, we have. Actually, we've had quite a lot."

"Oh. Because we're supposed to be pouring our bridge supports today as well and we've had sod all."

I said I'd investigate and give him a call back, but already the cogs in my brain were whirring around as to what possibly could have happened. As there were still a couple of mixer drivers on site who hadn't quite left yet, I collared one to see what was going on.

"Do you know anything about the deliveries to the other site today, mate?" I asked.

"...er, what other site?"

I asked him to get out the delivery paperwork he'd been given by his company so I could have a look. And there it was, clear as day... the name of the right building company, but the name of the site of the other bridge. No wonder we'd managed our pour so quick – we'd had their concrete as well as our own.

"You were supposed to go to the other site down the road with this. We've just had all their concrete!" I said to the driver.

"Oh," the driver replied, followed by a pause. "We were just told to drive down the main road and stop when we saw the signs for your company. No-one told us there were two sites. Sorry about that."

"Not your fault, fella," I replied. "You'd have thought they'd have known by now! Well, can you get back to the yard and pour some more for them?"

"No can do – we shut at lunchtimes on a Saturday. This is my last run. As soon as I get back to the yard, I'm going home. The offices will already be closed up until Monday morning."

Which left me to break the bad news to the other foreman and explain to him that not only had I inadvertently snaffled all his concrete, but that there wasn't going to be any concrete heading his way today at all. I felt bad enough as it was and apologised for the oversight – after all, it may have been a cock-up on the concrete company's part, but I should have been more thorough in checking the delivery notes. I guess that an easy thing to miss with so many mixers turning up and keeping me busy all morning.

I would have hated to be him: having to turn around and tell his men that they'd been sat around idle on site all morning and dragged away from their families on a Saturday for absolutely no reason. But not as much as I would have hated to have been the boss of the concrete company when our director rang him up come Monday morning...

SLEEPING ON THE JOB

Everyone has their old-fashioned preconceptions of workshy builders dozing in the sunshine all day and getting paid to do two-tenths of bugger all. And in a way, they're true. There aren't many builders around in my experience who can honestly put their hand on their heart and said they've never taken a sneaky nap or long lunch every now and again – I know I have.

Getting away with this sort of behaviour isn't easy, and needless to say, the consequences of getting caught can be severe... but also pretty hilarious at the same time, as I saw way back in the late Nineties on an office block project in central London.

The first odd thing about this job was that there was an extreme shortage of ladders. Now, stores getting raided for screws, bits of timber or cable ties and going short as a result happens all the time. But ladders? This was a strange one. There were apparently 50 ladders ordered onto the job, but whenever someone needed one to do some work at height, finding one was like finding hen's teeth. The management didn't have the foggiest idea where they'd all gone – and for that matter, neither did I.

All gradually became apparent one afternoon where one of the chippies was needed to join us for some really important shuttering work. Myself, my mate and the section foreman spent ages scouring the site for him, but despite the fact that he'd clocked in and so was definitely around somewhere, we just couldn't find him. No-one else on site said that they'd seen him since lunchtime.

The general foreman soon came hustling along and asked why we hadn't started this pour yet, and we explained that we were missing this particular bloke.

"Hang on a minute, I've got his mobile number," said the general foreman. "I'll give him a ring."

He found the bloke in his phone's contacts and dialled the number. After a few seconds, we could all hear the sound of a ringing phone, and judging from its clarity and its volume, it wasn't far from where we were all standing. It kept ringing, but we couldn't see anyone else around to answer it.

Then he realised that the noise was coming from immediately above his head. He looked up to find a long sheet of plywood balanced on the bottom sections of the RSJs that formed the main structure of the building, and this plywood was supported by some 4x2 timber. None of us had ever noticed it being there before, but we couldn't think why there would be any need for it to sit there with 4x2 support, two feet beneath the concrete ceiling atop the RSJ.

The phone was still ringing. We were all still looking up when, suddenly, a booted foot stuck out beyond the edge of the ply.

"OI!" bellowed the general foreman. "Get your arse down here now!"

A few seconds later, a ladder slid out from one side of the plywood and was lowered to the ground, shortly followed by an extremely sheepish builder clambering back down it to our level. It turns out he'd made himself a little hideaway up above everybody else, where he was able to have a nice snooze on the job completely undetected. Well, at least he would have been undetected if the dozy plank had remembered to put his phone on silent. He was sacked literally before his feet hit the ground.

After he'd trotted off down the road with his stuff, the proverbial lightbulb went on above the general foreman's head.

"Is this where all those fucking ladders have gone?!" he yelled. "How many more of these sleeping dens are there around here?"

I had no idea, because a) I never had any reason to have a good look up at study the ceiling above me, and b) if you'd set yourself up a secret sleeping den, you were hardly likely to blab it around site, were you?

Anyway, the next step was for the foreman to go around the rest of the site like a fine toothcomb, jabbing every bit of high-up plywood he could find with a long piece of waste timber he'd found lying around. Incredibly, there were around 30 of these things dotted all over the place. Any mutters or groans that were generated as a result of these jabs (and there were a few) immediately resulted as a sacking, but the majority just gave a secondary clunking noise. As it turned out, this meant that there was no-one up there at that time, but that a ladder had been left up there for access and safekeeping.

As one of the unlucky individuals (or stupid, depending on your viewpoint) descended after being caught in the act, the general foreman thought to ask him how he was able to get up to the top if the ladder was kept up there all the time.

"Have a look at that stick you're holding," said the now-unemployed bloke.

Affixed to one end was a long nail that came out a couple of inches from the timber and was then downwards by 90 degrees. This was the perfect angle to hook onto the bottom rung of a ladder above and pull it down, so that the sleepy builder could then climb up it and then pull the ladder back up behind himself to escape detection.

The general foreman stared utterly dumbfounded at this nail, realising that for weeks – months, for all he knew – he'd been paying dozens of workers to sleep on his site, and lost the use of a few dozen ladders, with absolutely no clue what was going on.

He kept himself quiet for a little while after that.

SACKED FROM THE SKY!

You know when you have that dream when you feel like you've woken up, and above you is the good Lord himself, beckoning you towards him and telling you that it's time for you to meet your maker? Well, imagine that happening in real life, but instead of it being Himself, it's actually a foreman beckoning you towards your P45 for having a snooze during a shift.

If you've read the story before this about sleeping on the job, then you won't be too surprised to learn that this incident happened on the same job and, funnily enough, involved the same general foreman. Strangely, it happened earlier than the previous story, so it wasn't like he was smarting from his missing blokes and ladders and had gone out in search of revenge. But his general demeanour and his antipathy towards blokes he found weren't doing a fair day's work for a fair day's pay made this an especially funny episode, and certainly one of the funniest things I've ever seen on a building site.

The three main concrete structures in the early stages of this office block job in London were, as is the case on many projects of its kind, the two lift shafts and the stairwell. They tend to go up first, ,with the RSJs to support each floor connected to them and the rest of the building basically working out from there. Anyway, the three shafts had been built near enough all the way to their peaks, and certainly far enough that the floorwork could begin on the lower levels, but there were still some blokes beavering away in the shafts to get them finished. Unfortunately, as you're about to discover, these blokes weren't exactly focused on getting work done.

To get up all that way, each shaft had a hoist attached to it: this is a temporary and very basic lift structure common on sites. It could take you up and down to whatever floor you wanted when you were in it, but unlike a normal lift, there was no means of commanding it to pick up anybody else from outside. So if someone else at the bottom needed to use it, they'd *rat-a-tat-tat* on the scaffolding to alert those above to send it back down. That was all well and good if you were only three or four floors up and could hear it, but this was a 14-floor building and there was no way you could hear from bottom to top.

The blokes working at the top of the three shafts quickly cottoned onto this, and realised that with no other access to them, they could do what they bloody well liked once they'd taken the hoist up until such time as they decided to come back down (normally for their lunch).

After a week or so, this was starting to cause serious problems to the operations below them as other blokes couldn't get about or move tools, plant or materials around site easily. The general foreman was alerted and was immediately – and as it turned out, rightly – suspicious that the chippies in the three shafts weren't doing much work up there. His solution turned out to be a stroke of genius. He radioed up to the crane driver and told him to get the man-rider ready.

A man-rider is, quite simply, a tall, thin metal cage which can be lifted up by a tower crane for transporting people anywhere they need to go on site. It's intended principally for transporting blokes up to high and/or inaccessible areas, and if you're not conversant with building sites and are trying to imagine what this looks like, then yes: it is absolutely as terrifying as it sounds. I'm not bad with heights myself but even I think twice about going into one of those. They are definitely not for the faint-hearted.

Whether or not heights were a problem for this general foreman didn't matter, though. He was clearly on a mission to catch these blokes. So into the man-rider he got and up he went into the London sky. Over the radio, he ordered the crane driver to hover him directly over the first lift shaft so he could see inside as the tops of them hadn't been done yet. And there he hit the jackpot: four blokes with helmets off, feet up, arms behind their heads basking in the sunshine while having a gentle doze. Which was promptly broken by an angry Irish foreman (as if this wasn't funny enough already), yelling:

"Ya feckin' lazy bastards! Get back down that hoist and feck aff home, ya lazy bunch of shoites!"

He was straight back onto the radio, which was on the common site channel so everyone could hear what was going on as it happened.

"OK, crane driver, take me over that other lift shaft, will ye?"

Across he went to find four more blokes sitting around, drinking tea and reading newspapers.

"Ya shower o' bastards! You're sacked, the lot o' ye!" came the cry, taking the kill count up to eight before he radioed back to the crane drive, calm and polite as you like:

"Now take me over the stairwell, please."

Preparing himself for a hat-trick, he was swung over to the stairwell to find that he couldn't see anyone working in there. That was because the top of the stairwell had been covered with a blue piece of plastic sheeting, apparently to keep the wind and rain out so the workers could stay dry. Everyone at ground level knew that this was bollocks, of course, and that those blokes had obviously had the brains to make sure no-one could see what they were doing, even from above.

Now, the foreman knew that they'd been slacking up there. We knew. And they themselves weren't stupid – they had enough sense to put the sheeting up, after all – so they must have known that they were under deep suspicion. But, for all that suspicion, they hadn't been caught and so there was no action the foreman could reasonably take against them.

What he could do, however, was order them to take down the sheeting, under the bullshit reasoning of it 'not being properly secured and so therefore would be a safety hazard was it to blow away'. Knowing their card was marked, they took the sheeting down and got back to the work they were supposed to do, making doubly sure they finished up there before they got rained on.

So in the end, the foreman could still claim a 2-1 victory, and I'm sure he felt very smug about his achievements when he sat down for his pint of Guinness that evening. From my perspective, after so many years in the trade, you get to the point where you think you've seen it all. But nothing can prepare you for seeing a raging Irishman swinging around off a tower crane about 200 feet in the air.

THE CARPETBAGGERS

This story is probably more suited to one of those consumer shows on the telly like *Watchdog* or *Rip-Off Britain*, but as I don't have Anne Robinson or Gloria Hunniford's mobile numbers immediately to hand, I guess this audacious tale of theft on a grand scale will have to sit in here.

One of my very first jobs in the trade, way back in the late Seventies (yes, I am that old, stop sniggering at the back there) was doing various bits of internal fitting for a public body in central London. It was a big organisation with offices and departments dotted all over the capital, and one week we were required to fit some new carpets on one of the higher floors of the main headquarters building. The facilities department – or 'maintenance', as it was called in the good old days – was based in a different building about two miles away, and so had left us some instructions at the building we were working on and left us to get on with it.

Being a public body and being long before the age of austerity, this wasn't just your usual squares of piss-thin office carpet that you get nowadays. It was thick stuff in long rolls and looked absolutely beautiful. It might have been an Axminster, but to be honest I can't remember exactly. But anyway, over a couple of days the gang of us moved the desks and chairs around as we fitted each length of roll, worked our way across this big open-plan expanse and eventually put the furniture back where it was. That then left us a couple more days to do the tricky bits that needed more skilful work, like getting the carpet down around doorways, radiator pipes and the like.

It was just as we were finishing this off on the Thursday afternoon that a couple of blokes with overalls and a clipboard turned up to have a look at the installation. It was clear from their facial expression that they weren't particularly impressed with something. We worked out that they were from the carpet supplier.

"I don't know how this has happened, boys, but you've fitted completely the wrong type of carpet," said one of them. "Sorry about that."

"What do you want us to do, then?" asked our gang leader.

"Well, we haven't got a van with us to take it all away now and we won't be able to get one over here until Monday morning. I tell you what: get it all rolled up again and leave it downstairs by reception. We'll come and collect it first thing Monday and should be back with you later in the day with the proper carpet."

It sounded like the most common-sense solution to all of us, so the overall-wearing blokes left us to it and we spent the remainder of the week getting it all back up off the floor and down into reception, where it was cordoned off ready for the collection on

Monday. It all seemed very organised and seemed to make sense, so our gang leader saw no need to call the maintenance office as, in his eyes, they must have arranged it all. As you're about to discover, not making that call proved to be a huge mistake.

The weekend passed by and as we reported for duty on Monday morning, we came into reception to find that that, as promised, the old carpet had been collected up and taken away. In the meantime, as we waited for the new stuff to arrive, we found ourselves other jobs to be getting on with in other departments. The rest of Monday passed, with no sign of the new carpet... as did Tuesday. And Wednesday.

By Thursday morning, our gang leader thought he'd best give the maintenance boys a call and see where this new carpet was. Slightly bemused at the request – understandably, as it was the first they'd heard of the problem – they said they'd get onto the carpet company and find out. Later that day, the response came back: there was no replacement carpet ordered, the first carpet they sent out was indeed the correct one, they had no idea why we'd been asked to take that carpet up, and on no account had they sent out any blokes in overalls or otherwise last week.

The absolute disaster of a situation was unravelling before our eyes: two men, posing as workers from the carpet supply company, had spun us an elaborate story that had allowed them to turn up with their van on the Monday morning and steal all the carpet.

All the gaps in this incredible story were filled in a week or so later, when we were sat down for a briefing with the maintenance department, the carpet supply company and the police. It transpired that we were just the latest victim in a spate of similar carpet thefts that were sweeping the capital, and what we discovered was that these cheeky buggers would tell the unsuspecting workers that they'd be back in a few days to collect the rolls of carpet rather than pick it up at the time.

This not only sounded so plausible and sensible that no-one ever felt the need to check with their maintenance departments that it was all above board, but it also gave the crims a weekend to find a willing buyer for the carpet. This meant that they could rock up on Monday morning, collect the carpet that had been neatly placed in reception for them, and drive it straight over to the buyer and install it that day, ensuring that they never had any evidence on them should they ever be caught.

Apparently, in the 12 months prior to us being done over for it, there had been dozens of similar instances in London. All of them were in buildings of big companies where the maintenance department was based off-site, so that there was never anyone immediately on hand to check things out. It really was amazing stuff. Of course, in the modern era of mobile phones, emails, CCTV and the like, it'd be far easier these days to verify these guys' identities and stories, but it was a very different time with very different attitudes back then.

Ultimately, the maintenance department had to suck it up and shell out for another new carpet. And second time round, they made damned sure that they were on hand to rubber-stamp it once we'd laid it.

DUCTING FOR COVER

It's funny to think of some of the stories you pick up third, fourth or even fifth-hand just through hearing gossip from other people. It's normally pretty easy to tell the difference between a yarn that's totally true and one that's been spun up out of all realistic proportion. Stereotypically, the place where builders are most likely to pick up on these tales is the old greasy spoon cafe, but on one particular job in the Midlands, I learnt first-hand over a number of weeks about a cheeky bit of sleight of hand pulled by a subcontractor.

I was working on putting together some new retail units, a job that went on for several months, and every morning I'd break for breakfast at a caff over the road. After a while, I'd got to know some other workers who took their breakfast there every day, too. They were contracted out to work their way around all the roads in the area, putting in new metal ducting under the pavements for telecoms cabling and the like to be guided through. Basically, they were going along manholes spaced at regular intervals along the pavement, pitting in boxes for access so that the telecoms guys could feed the cabling through later, and they were also digging up the pavement to put in the tunnelling. All common stuff, but a big job given the number of roads they'd been given to work on.

There were four or five of these blokes most days, and they worked for a small sub-contractor that I'd never heard of before. After about six weeks, I'd got to know them really well and could happily talk news, weather, football and the like with them over a fry-up and a cup of tea.

Then, one Monday, they didn't come in, which I thought a little odd, something that seemed more odd as the rest of the week wore on without them appearing. It occurred to me that I'd normally see their vans out and about on the roads around our site most days, but I hadn't seen those either. It was as if they'd vanished off the face of the Earth.

I knew that the owner of the caff was a 'sociable sort' (builders' slang for 'a gossip') so I thought I'd ask him what had been going on.

"I'm not sure, Barry," he said. "But I tell you one thing that was strange: a load of telecoms engineers came in earlier in the week and they were moaning like hell about not being able to get their cabling done. I wonder if it was something to do with that. If I see them in here again, I'll point them out to you."

After that, I didn't really think much of the whole thing for a while. But a couple of weeks further down the line, the caff owner duly pointed the cabling guys out to me, so I thought I'd say hello and see if I could get more information out of them.

"Ah, you noticed they'd suddenly disappeared as well, did you?" one of them said. "If I could get hold of them, I'd tear the bastards limb from limb."

"Bloody hell, steady on!" I said. "I'd got to know those blokes pretty well and they seemed pretty decent to me. What could they have done to you?"

He then promptly launched into a long-winded story about what these blokes had done, interspersed with a lot of swearing, questioning of parentage and threats of GBH.

"You see those bits out there that they dug up?" he said, pointing outside to a strip of re-laid pavement that those subbies had put down to cover their work from a few weeks previously. "They aren't real."

"What do you mean they aren't real?" I said, completely baffled.

"Well, they were going through each manhole, putting the steel boxes in so that we could feed the cabling through to the next box 50 metres down the pavement," he went on. "But when we got to the first one, we found we couldn't feed the cable through more than a couple of metres before we hit a complete blockage. We went down to the next one to see if we could get through from the other end, but had the same problem, again after about two metres or so."

"At both ends? That sounds odd!" I said, still completely flummoxed.

"You can say that again. Anyway, we tried to shine a torch down there to see what the blockage was, but the angle of the manhole made it too hard to see. So we called in another bloke who has a light and a CCTV camera that we could drop into the manholes. Which we did, and when we looked at what was causing the blockage, all we could see was soil. And it was the same at the second manhole, too."

It was at this point that the scales finally fell from my eyes.

"You're not saying that they'd put the manhole boxes in, but never bothered to do the ducting with it?" I asked.

"Got it in one, mate," said the bloke, exasperatedly. "It turns out they'd dug up the street where the ducting should have been laid, but only did a couple of inches and then recovered it again with new asphalt, so that it looked like they'd done the job they were supposed to."

I couldn't believe what I was hearing.

"So then what happened?"

"Well, the thing is that these subbies were getting paid weekly for this work, mainly because they were such a small company. So our firm was paying out for work, than on basic inspection by our clerk of works, looked like it was complete from surface level. But after six weeks of pulling this scam, they obviously decided that they'd been riding their luck for long enough without getting caught, and so they scarpered. No-one from our company has seen or heard from any of them since and they can't track them down. They've earned tens of thousands of pounds between them for ducting work they didn't do."

"Fucking hell, they could have all run away to Barbados by now!" I said. And for all I know to this day, they might well have.

HELL HATH NO FURY…

There's nothing worse on a building site than a mouthy bastard that thinks he's God's gift to construction and spends his days lording it over everyone by shouting. To be honest, that probably isn't specific to the building trade: I reckon there's probably at least one cock like that in every workplace in the land.

Now, I can tolerate that kind of behaviour if a bloke can walk the walk as well as talking the talk, and over the years I've been extremely fortunate enough to have worked on a few jobs where that's been the case with the foremen. The best ones are normally hard bastards who will give you a bollocking if you deserve one, but that will treat you fairly too. In those cases, I don't mind their bullshit as much.

One example of where this was categorically not the case, however, came the thick end of 20 years ago, when I was working on the construction of a section of shopping centre in the town in which I live. Having got used to the drudgery (and eye-watering expense even then) of commuting into London by rail for many of my jobs, to work on this project just a short drive from my house was bliss. It meant I could get up a lot later, get home a lot earlier and not spend two hours a day with my face pressed up to a train window while I'm suffocated by other people's farts. It also meant I was earning a lot more in real terms because I wasn't shelling out for a season ticket for the train, as well as having the ability to nip home for my lunch rather than stump up for canteen food.

Well, actually, the last point is right in principle but wasn't the case here, because this job featured the best canteen food I've ever experienced on a building site. It was just as it used to be on sites: a family catering operation made up of a mother managing her daughters, rather than the corporate outsourced rubbish that's ten-a-penny on sites nowadays.

This particular family were Irish, and headed by a lovely lady who I'll call Mary. Every day they'd have special meals available beyond the normal fare of fry-ups, burger meals and so on. These specials were proper home-cooked, home-prepared stuff like Irish stews. The food was so good that instead of earing at home, I had no hesitation in spending the extra cash to be served a good hearty meal with a cheery smile from Mary and her daughters.

For me, and indeed for most of the guys on site, this was just fine and dandy. But there's always one loudmouth git that has to let the side down, and in this case it was our foreman. We have a saying in our trade: 'There's three ways of doing things: the right way, the wrong way and the foreman's way'. But with this bloke, you could forget even trying to do things the right way and God help you if you did something the wrong way.

In reality, he was a poor manager, happy to wash his dirty linen in public, he bollocked people for mistakes in front of their co-workers, and was stubbornly pig-headed in his refusal to accept that anyone's ideas could be good unless they were his.

Anyway, one lunchtime we all filed into the canteen to get our lunch from Mary, but due to the sheer popularity of the place, there was a little bit of a wait on the food. Most of us were happy to quietly wait our turn (the food was worth it, after all) but this foreman insisted on voicing his displeasure at the wait in a loud enough voice that everyone could hear.

"This is shit," he'd moan. "I'm a busy man, I've got work to do! Why can't they get the bloody hell on with it?"

This went on for a few minutes as the queue edged forward, and while I was in no doubt that Mary could full well hear what he was saying as she served the blokes further up, she ignored him and cheerfully carried on with her job. At least she did until the foreman came to be served. He ordered the stew, which Mary carefully ladled into a bowl and handed over to him.

"Here you go, my love" she said.

"What the fucking hell is this?" the foreman bawled as he completely lost his rag. "You've made me wait 15 fucking minutes to be served this slop? It looks like you've spooned this up out of the fucking khazi outside."

The canteen fell completely silent. Everyone knew that he was massively out of order, but as he was the boss and was obviously in a mood, no-one was going to get involved. Mary said nothing. All she did was stare blankly at him for a few seconds… before leaning over the counter and slamming her clenched and ringed right fist straight into his jaw, flooring him with a single punch.

There was no cheer or applause from the blokes, who sat there, mouths wide open, watching this unfold. The reaction was more like the collective intake of breath you get when you hire a plumber and he claps eyes on your dodgy pipes or your water leak.

The foreman pulled himself to his feet and staggered out of the canteen without a word, and after a few seconds, Mary turned to the next bloke in the queue, switched her smile back on and beamed:

"What'll it be, my love?"

We didn't see the foreman again that day, and we expected him to look pretty red-faced when he rolled in the next morning. But as it turned out, he didn't turn up for work that morning, and as a matter of fact was never seen on that job again. I guess the embarrassment of getting called out on his arseyness and getting knocked to the floor by an Irishwoman in her late fifties must have been too much for him.

It was his own fault. You can criticise near enough anyone you want for virtually anything and probably not face any consequences. But have a pop at a mother for her cooking skills and be prepared to go down like a sack of spuds.

MIND THE MEAT AND TWO!

Back in the 1970s, I did my apprenticeship based around south-west London with one of the country's biggest construction firms. I won't say exactly which one for obvious reasons, but they're still going strong today. It was an eye opening experience at the time, for a teenager like me living in the smoke and learning all the valuable lessons about construction the hard way. It was tough at times, but as well as teaching me things which are still useful for my work four decades on, it was also a helluva lot of fun.

A lot of the more entertaining moments came when everyone came to let their hair down at the end of the year. Now, we've all got our own stories to tell about people who have made dicks of themselves at the office Christmas party, but this was the 1970s and things were a bit different back then.

With this company, the Christmas dos always great affairs: enjoyable social occasions without the sole emphasis on getting blind drunk that seems to prevail at these events so much these days. And their seasonal soirees had an extra-special touch to them.

They were hosted on a party boat that would cruise at slow speed up and down the River Thames for the evening, stopping along the way at a selection of DSS clubs (that's Divorced, Separated and Single for you youngsters).

As the evening progressed, everyone had a great time, enjoying themselves and having a good laugh before we all headed back to our respective homes for the Christmas and New Year shutdown. It was towards the end of the evening, as a few people were getting a bit too merry, that one unforgettable incident occurred.

I was stood with a couple of fellow apprentice mates in a corridor of the boat, each of us with a can of lager on the go, and near where we were stood was the door to one of the toilets on board. No-one was really taking much notice of it – we weren't waiting to use the loo at the time – and were deep in conversation when suddenly, there was an almighty crash as the door flew open.

Out came a woman of around 40 in a certain state of undress, holding up the top part of her dress to keep her bosom away from prying eyes as she ran off in tears. Left in the toilet was our boss, a man of around 50, clearly dishevelled, a bit dazed and with his flies open.

"What happened, guv?" one of my mates asked.

"I'd brought her in here for a bit of 'fun' and everything was going fine," he replied. "Then I put my hand up her skirt, and…"

"What?" I pressed.

"…and grabbed hold of her meat and two. Well, 'his' meat and two, I suppose."

"You're not saying she's a bloke?!" I gasped. "We

saw you on the dancefloor in the last club. You've had your tongue down her – sorry, his – bloody throat all night!"

"Don't you think I fucking well know that?" he growled in reply.

It was at this point where he found that my two mates were literally crying and rolling around on the floor with laughter. And as it sunk in just what had happened, I found it increasingly difficult to stifle the laughter myself.

"Shut the fuck up, the lot of you," he snarled. "Any word of this to anybody and I'll sack you on the spot." He then slammed the door back shut so he could put his mouse back into the house and make himself respectable again.

As the three of us chuckled to ourselves, we went back out into the main dancefloor area to be confronted by some of the girls from the office, mainly receptionists and typists as it was back then.

"What the hell happened there? Is this something one of you have done to the poor girl?" asked the most senior of them.

"We can't really say, but it was nothing to do with us." I replied.

"All I know is that poor girl has gone off crying. We couldn't even grab her to find out what on Earth was wrong."

"Can you keep a secret?"

"Go on, what is it?" she said, despite being well-known as the biggest gossip in the company.

"The boss just got caught in the toilets with her and grabbed the full set up her skirt. She's a man," I told her.

The receptionist stopped for a second as the

implications of this whirred round in her head.

"So, that girl was actually a bloke wearing women's clothes?" she eventually said to me.

"Yup. Guess he didn't spot the Adam's apple while he was giving her a snog on the dancefloor."

"Well, I'll be," came the reply from the perplexed old dear. "That explains everything."

"What do you mean?"

"Well if she was actually a man, then no wonder we couldn't catch her when she ran off!"

Postscript (as if you thought this couldn't get any better!): come the first Monday in January, everyone had come back into work but certainly hadn't forgotten what had gone on aboard that boat. Quite the reverse: the story had spread like wildfire.

Our boss was back in work, carrying on as if nothing had happened. And an uneasy truce was just about holding within the office. At least it did until breakfast time, when everyone filed into the canteen.

As the boss got to the front of the queue for his fry-up, he found himself in front of the canteen woman. Six foot tall, middle-aged and Irish, she said what she thought and she wasn't a woman to be trifled with.

The moment she realised who she was serving, she bellowed, in the loudest voice she could: "Do you want a sausage and two plum tomatoes with your breakfast, my dear?"

The canteen erupted into hysterics, and the boss quietly took his breakfast and sat down to eat it, without a word... but with a face as red as, well, a plum tomato.

LE TOUR DE SITE

This one isn't a blunder as such, but I thought I'd include it, just to show that every now and again, even builders have strokes of luck.

I was working as an agency foreman on the expansion of a big out-of-town rctail park. This placc was big enough as it was, but was getting so many customers every day - think coachloads of Chinese tourists with bundles of cash to spend - that they could make millions by making it even bigger.

The scale of the job made the site, in terms of its physical size, one of the biggest I've ever worked on. I rocked up on my first morning to find, annoyingly but unsurprisingly, that my offices were tucked away right at one end of the site.

You can probably guess what's coming next, so no prizes for this one: the particular bit of work I was overseeing was right at the other end of the site. It was the thick end of a mile away.

Now, I'm not a fat bastard by any means, but I'm not getting any younger and I've put on a bit of a beer belly since I came off the tools and became a foreman. So a 15-20 minute walk each way from office to work area gave me a much-needed bit of regular exercise.

But nonetheless, it was an enormous pain in the arse, to the point where it was making my job really difficult to do. If I sat in the office all day, I was detached from what the blokes on the tools were doing, but if I stayed down in the work area, then I couldn't fill in paperwork and the like. And if I tried to mix the two, I wasted half the sodding day just walking back and forth and never got anything useful done at all. It was a bloody nightmare.

To try and solve the problem, I asked the site director if I could get the use of a van. I'm not one to try and grab hold of any perk going whether I need it or not, but I felt this was essential to do my job properly. In typical director style, the answer came back: "We'll sort you one out tomorrow, Barry."

I've been in this game long enough to know that when your boss promises you something 'tomorrow', then that 'tomorrow' is unlikely to arrive. Ever. Even so, after a week or so of constant promises but no transport forthcoming, I was starting to consider jacking it in and trying my luck on finding another job somewhere else. I just couldn't keep traipsing up and down like the Changing of the bloody Guard for weeks on end.

And, then, as I was plodding my way back down to the work area yet again, there it was. Hidden in a hedge on the site boundary, completely out of anyone's sight, the answer to my prayers caught the corner of my eye. And as long as I have a hole in my arse, I don't think I'll ever again be as happy to find an abandoned bicycle.

In fairness, while that makes it sound like I'd stumbled upon some trick piece of kit, Chris Froome's spare ride it most certainly wasn't. First of all, it was an old mountain bike, of the kind normally flogged out cheap by the supermarkets at Christmas and nicked by some scrote by New Year. Secondly, it was a girl's bike: low crossbar and everything. And thirdly, it had seen better days: the tyres were flat, the gears wouldn't change and the chain was rusty. But let's face it, I wasn't looking for anything special. And it was dumped in a hedge, after all.

I left it where it was for the time being, and in my lunch break nipped into town to the pound shop. £2 later, and armed with a pump and a puncture repair kit, I was soon back on site trying to make this thing vaguely rideable.

As it turned out, the tyres weren't punctured and just needed a bit of a boost. So within a few minutes, I was riding around nice and easy on the one gear out of 18 that it insisted on staying in. It wasn't fast, but it'd do two or (at a push) three times walking pace no problem - and that was all I needed it to do.

As I coasted into the work area on it for the first time, the looks on the lads' faces were priceless. Then came the banter: "Where's your basket?", "I didn't know you rode side-saddle, Barry!" and so on.

But I think they knew how much of a difference it was going to make their lives just as much as mine. Being able to get from office to work area in five minutes rather than 15 was really helpful for me giving out instructions and making sure they were all on the right track.

But nothing could compare with the reaction I got when I rode it back to the office. I'd parked it at the bottom of the external stairs, this being one of those offices made of out Portakabins. And I'd been back in the office about two minutes when the director - the very man who couldn't get me a van sorted - thundered into the room.

"WHICH ONE OF YOU TOSSERS HAS PARKED A FUCKING GIRL'S BIKE AT THE BOTTOM OF THE FUCKING STAIRS?!"

I wasn't going to say anything, but the smug grin on my face gave my game away pretty quickly. And once he saw it was me, and realised that I was riding it because he couldn't get his arse in gear sorting me a van out, he stopped dead in his tracks. After a few seconds of considered thought, he grunted: "Just keep it out of sight, Barry, all right?" and scuttled off.

As the great Alan Partridge was always so fond of saying: "Needless to say, I had the last laugh!" But it just goes to show that there's always a light at the end of the tunnel, even on the shittiest of jobs.

And as for the bike? Well, after giving it a new lease of life for a couple of months, I didn't really want to part with it when the job was completed. I guess I'm a soppy old fool at heart.

So on my last day, I loaded it into the back of my car and drove it home. It now lives in my garage alongside my own bike, and every so often gets a run out to the pub when a relative or a friend comes to visit. When presented with it to ride on, they always ask: "Where the fuck did you get this piece of shit from?". But, to be fair, they always laugh when I tell them this story.

ANYONE FOR ICE CREAM?

Working in construction generally means that we don't deal with members of the public very often. At least that's the theory, anyway. When we do, that normally means that something has happened that shouldn't have. And on one particular occasion, that meant an unlikely public safety issue and an intervention from the boys in blue.

I was overseeing a section of motorway that was being converted into what they call a 'smart motorway.' If you've been on the motorways lately, then you'll know what that means: one lane cordoned off for works with a Variguard barrier. Meanwhile, the rest of the traffic is squeezed into three ridiculously narrow lanes, complete with a 50mph limit and average speed cameras everywhere.

These sites are just as much of a ballache to work on as they are to drive through. Working on a site that's several miles long means you get ferried out to where you're working by minibus, and you get picked up again at the end of your shift in the same way. Once you're out there, you're out there for the day.

At regular intervals along the way, there are small Portakabins used as break rooms, so at least you have somewhere to relax away from the roar of the motorway traffic. Food is brought to you in the form of snack wagons that crawl along the working lane, and on this job there were two: one selling hot food, and one selling cold food.

Inevitably, one was always more popular than the other, varying according to the weather and the time of year. This especially applied in the summer, as the cold food vehicle was an ice-cream van.

On a particularly hot day one August, the ice-cream van was doing a roaring trade, with pretty much every bloke on site outside and savouring a 99 as the temperatures soared into the thirties. But after a while, we noticed a load of shouting, and we soon realised it was coming in our direction.

Because of an accident further up the road, the motorway was at a complete halt. Nobody likes being sat in a car on a scorching hot day in the middle of a traffic jam. And when you feel like the roadworks are already wasting your time, looking out of your window to see a load of builders stood around eating ice creams is only going to piss you off even more.

Motorists were yelling at us and taking photos on their phones, no doubt to be posted to social media, but there was nothing we could do. We couldn't get back to work because we needed materials… which couldn't reach us because of that very same jam.

A couple of hundred yards further up the road, however, the reaction of the public was very different. The ice-cream van had stopped to serve the next working gang, but was also being mobbed by motorists who were getting out of their cars and climbing over the Variguard to get some cold refreshments for themselves.

Having members of the public climb into a live building site - even one where work has come to a stop - is obviously dangerous in itself. But then, suddenly, it got much worse. With the accident up ahead having been cleared away, the traffic started moving again.

This led to the hilarious sight of several Joe and Jane Bloggses playing chicken across the motorway, darting through moving traffic as they legged it back to their cars with two ice creams in each hand. Thankfully, they all got back without being hit (and more importantly, without any Flakes being dislodged) and we all thought that was that.

That was until about five minutes later when the police arrived, right next to the ice-cream van. And this was proper Plod, not the traffic womble Plod you see putting a million and one cones out at the first sign of a crisis.

I discovered later that there was a short 'exchange of views' between the ice-cream man and the policemen. It turned out that the whole incident had been seen on CCTV and had caused all sorts of alerts and mass panic at the command centre.

The ice-cream man was then told in no uncertain terms to get on up the road, and not sell any more ice creams that day. Once he'd cleared off, Plod got back in their car and sped off, and at the same time our materials turned up and we could get back to work.

The next day was just as hot and we were all looking forward to getting another ice cream. But as breaktime arrived and the hot snack wagon rolled in, the ice-cream van was nowhere to be seen.

"Where's your mate with the ice cream?" I asked the wagon driver.

"He's had his permit to work on the motorway revoked," came the reply. "Apparently having an ice-cream van on the motorway works counts as a public health hazard. Funny that..."

FEELING A BIT FLAT

Foremen aren't as bright as they like to think they are. Christ, I became one, so it can't be that hard to do! Seriously, though, a lot of foremen like the ego boost that comes with being able to swan around site being Bertie Big-Bollocks. As a result, any time their lack of skills or intelligence get publicly shown up, they tend to react pretty badly.

The problem is that builders tend to be sarky sods at the best of times and never pass up an opportunity to take the piss out of someone or knock a bloke off his high horse. So every day on sites up and down the land, foremen get wound up, and blokes end up getting themselves into all sorts of trouble.

The example of this behaviour that I'm going to share here is so biblically fucking stupid that you wouldn't have thought it was remotely possible. But honest to God, it really did happen.

This central London job around the turn of the millennium involved building lots of high-rise tower blocks. Because of the scale of the project, there were half a dozen tower cranes on site. The general foreman, however, had a major bee in his bonnet about tower cranes. He hated them when they weren't doing anything because it was a waste of resources, but he also hated them when materials were hanging off them, going off on half-cocked rants like: "What the fuck's that doing on that fucking crane?!"

One day, one of the cranes had broken down with some sort of mechanical fault, and was left with its jib raised up, as cranes always are when they aren't being used. Like each of the others, this crane had its own driver, as well as its own banksman who would direct the picking up and dropping off of various loads into different places. But with no work to do, they parked themselves in the canteen while they waited for the crane repair crew to arrive on site.

This foreman was already pissed off enough that the crane was out of action. But when he found out that it meant he had two blokes reading the paper in the canteen and getting paid for it, this pissed him off even more. So he quickly went to find them and give them a good bollocking, just as the rest of us were filing in for our usual breaktime.

"What the fuck are you two doing in here?" he yelled, in front of all of us. "I don't pay you to sit about drinking fucking tea!"

The driver calmly replied: "We're in here because the crane's broken down."

"So what's fucking wrong with it?"

"It's got a puncture."

"Well get the fucking tyre fitters out here and get the fucking thing fixed, then!" And at that, the foreman turned on his heels and walked straight out of the canteen.

Before I continue, take a minute to go back,

re-read that particular exchange and take in what was actually said.

Yup, that's right. With a face as straight as a laser-guided level, they told him that the tower crane - you know, one of those 200ft-high bastards that's concreted into place - had a flat tyre. And the foreman was so blindly angry to listen to what was said that he believed them!

Obviously, it wasn't going to be long before he'd realised what a complete tit he'd just made of himself and come looking for retribution. So about five seconds after he left, everyone in the canteen that had witnessed this, including these two blokes, scarpered bloody pronto.

And sure enough, about another 30 seconds later, the penny finally dropped and the foreman realised that a) tower cranes don't have wheels, and b) he had made himself look a prize twat in front of dozens of people supposedly less talented and less intelligent than he was. We all knew the penny had dropped because we heard him running around site, ranting and raving his head off.

In those days, general foreman, and in particular the old-school Irish ones like this one, didn't like the 'ground troops' getting one over on them. Because, more often than not, the news of what had happened in London would travel like wildfire back over the Irish Sea to all the other builders 'back home'.

Soon enough, all his mates and contacts would be sending him texts like: 'I know a good tyre fitter for you' literally within minutes. And if you're a bloke with a big ego, finding out you're being laughed at in two different countries at the same time can come as a bit of a shock to say the least.

Of course, I don't know this international piss-takery happened for sure, because I've obviously not had access to his texts or his voicemail. But my gut instinct tells me that it's definitely what happened here. Why? Because for three days afterwards, paralysed by an embarrassment-induced rage, this foreman was like a bear with a sore head to anyone and everyone he could lay his hands on.

In fact, when one of the crane repair crew strode into the canteen the following morning and announced he was 'here to fix the flat tyre', he had to take swift evasive action to avoid a tea mug that had been promptly launched towards his skull.

The moral of this story is simple. However much you might want to take the piss out of a foreman, and however much of an arsehole he may or may not be, it is never, ever worth it. Because they're in charge, and don't you bloody well forget it.

THE TALE OF BLONDIE BILL

This is my last story, and by this point you probably think I've got some sort of vendetta against the Irish, given the number of stories I've told that highlight their pig-headedness.

Honestly, nothing could be further from the truth. Most of my best times on sites, and some of the most rewarding jobs I've worked on, have been run by Irish foremen and populated by Irish workers. Indeed, my best mate from the building trade, who I've been going around sites with for the best part of 20 years, is an Irishman (hello, Pat!). It's just that it isn't half funny when they make complete and utter bellends of themselves.

And so to finish, I'm going to tell you all about Blondie Bill. That isn't his real identity, as I'm sure you've guessed, but it's an adaptation of a nickname that everyone knew him by. But he was an extremely experienced foreman that was well-known on the London scene at the time. I would say he had a no-nonsense reputation, but to be fair, all foremen do.

I came across him on a hotel construction job near

one of the big London rail terminals. This was back in the early Nineties: the 'good old days' when you could get overtime on a Saturday, work until 1:00pm and get a full day's pay for it. It was always worth doing to get plenty of pub money for the rest of the weekend.

One particular Saturday, I was set to be putting some shutters together for some concrete to be poured on this hotel job, at what is known as 'podium level'. This is basically the first level above the ground floor, where extra formwork is needed to separate the normal hotel rooms from the hustle and bustle of reception, the restaurant and the bar below.

The stores, where all the materials were kept, were on the ground floor, and to do this fiddly bit of shuttering, I had to use these little fittings. They were supplied loose and they'd easily be lost in a pocket or my toolbox, so as I came onto site this Saturday morning, I went to the stores first to get enough to last me the day. Handily, I'd stopped off at a coffee shop for a cup of tea just before I came on site, and I thought it'd be good use of the empty paper cup to carry all of these fittings. So I filled it up and carried it upstairs to the podium level.

Getting these fittings, combined with a few other bits of titting about, meant I was a bit late in getting to my work area. Ninety-nine times out of 100, this wouldn't be a problem and no-one would bat much of an eyelid, especially as I'd clocked into site on time. But sod's law dictated that this was the one time that I got caught for it.

From the other side of the podium level, Blondie Bill shouted at me:

"Oi! We start here at fucking eight, not fucking half-eight."

I replied: "Bloody hell, calm down! I was next to you in the bloody changing room getting changed at quarter to eight. What's the big problem?"

Of course, as I'm sure you've come to appreciate by now, arguing back against a shouty foreman is always a bad idea. This was doubly so on a Saturday morning when Blondie Bill had more than likely had a good session on the Guinness on the Friday night.

He then yelled back, having spotted my coffee cup: "Well maybe if you weren't fucking around buying poncey coffee, you wouldn't have been so late getting up here. Pack up your tools and fuck off home! You're sacked!"

Unperturbed by this (there was plenty of other work around to pay the bills, after all), I picked up the coffee cup, turned it upside-down, and all the little fittings it contained showered onto the floor. Without a word, and without waiting for his or anybody else's reaction, I picked up my tools, grabbed my clothes from the changing room and caught the train home. Mentally, I just wrote off the whole thing as just another dickhead foreman incident, and thought that was the end of the matter.

Now, back then, most of the foremen from this company working on various sites around London would finish their half-days on Saturday mornings and then meet up in a pub for the afternoon. As these foremen were almost exclusively Irish in origin or descent, the pub was in that Irish-heavy pocket of north-west London around Harrow and Kilburn.

Years later, thanks to an old friend I caught up with on another job, I found out that on this day, Blondie Bill walked into this Irish pub and joined three other foremen at the bar.

The barman said: "D'ya want your usual, Bill?"

"Yes, please," came the reply.

Soon enough, a nice steaming hot cup of coffee - in a takeaway plastic cup, no less - was placed in front of him on the bar.

The other foremen found this highly amusing, the old rumour mill having already filled them in on his run-in with me before they'd even got to the pub. Blondie Bill, of course, didn't see the funny side. And I'm sure he'd have given me all sorts of shit had I ever come across him on another job further down the line. Thank Christ I didn't!

POSTSCRIPT

As you've now read (and hopefully enjoyed), I've seen plenty of funny stuff on sites over these last 40 years. But construction is a serious business, and in that time I've seen the industry change virtually beyond recognition. And not necessarily for the better.

Make no mistake: building sites in Britain today are far, far safer than they were when I started out as an apprentice in the late Seventies. The general philosophy of 'health and safety' has forced a positive cultural change across large parts of the industry. Because of this, countless accidents and injuries have been prevented and countless lives have been saved. Without a doubt, it's the single greatest thing that's happened within the industry during my career.

The problem is that, in my opinion, 'health and safety' has been taken way too far, and the whole point of the exercise has been drowned in a sea of paperwork and red tape. It's no longer about making sure everyone is safe, as it was originally. It's now about companies covering their backs and making sure they don't get sued or penalised when stuff goes wrong. The industry as a whole - and perhaps British society as a whole - has lost sight of what health and safety is supposed to be about.

This lack of focus on personal safety is made even worse in the current environment, where the vast majority of workers are agency-based and self-employed like myself, moving from job to job frequently and easily. It means that anyone who rocks the boat with the client company's management about grievances, safety issues or whatever is simply going to be booted out. Seen as a troublemaker and a pain in the arse, they're invariably replaced with someone a bit more, shall we say, 'co-operative'.

What's more, if auditors or assessors uncover a particular failing when they come to visit, then they want 'action' to be taken. That basically means sacking someone, and that inevitably ends up being the scapegoat agency worker because they're the easiest to sack. This attitude, allied to the lack of contracted workers staying with one company for any long period of time, means there is no culture of safety or practical improvement. In fact, the system as it is now works actively against it.

In the meantime, another change has happened within the make-up of the workforce that is putting people at unnecessary risk: the wide range of different nationalities of builder that have migrated into this country over the last 15 to 20 years.

It's a strange paradox that in the old days, we had very little paperwork but everyone spoke, understood and read English very well. That was because the furthest away any migrant workers came from was basically Donegal or County Kerry. But now, we have masses of paperwork and written material, but significant numbers of workers on site from Asia, Eastern Europe, Africa or wherever who don't understand verbal or written instructions in English. I'm not necessarily against these workers coming over to try and earn a better living for themselves and their families, but it's not right when a lack of language skills ends up putting everyone at risk.

A perfect example of this disconnect happens on sites day-in, day-out during 'Toolbox Talks'. These are short presentations covering particular practical or safety issues, ranging from hot weather and taking on fluids to wood cutting safety, and everything in between. When done properly, they're really useful and one of the best modern developments in how construction sites operate. When they aren't, they're a fucking waste of time, especially when complicated issues are covered to a workforce with a poor command of English.

On one job, I saw one local bloke get bollocked for reading a newspaper during the toolbox talk. He pointed out that there was no difference between him not paying attention and the ten new Indian blokes on his left staring blankly at the speaker, because they didn't understand what was going on and no-one was translating for them. But there wasn't any real action taken, because the company needed the Indian blokes' skills and manpower.

In reality, all you need to succeed on any site is a good gang of workers - regardless of nationality - all putting a shift in and working together as a team, while understanding and complementing each other's skills and abilities. You'd think that was basic common sense, but that tends to be an exception rather than the norm.

The lack of English of some of the migrant workforce doesn't help this, but the structure and recruitment that happens at the upper levels of the industry today is just as much to blame. Nowhere is this more apparent than with the current generation of engineers. I fucking hate modern engineers.

When I first started, engineers were older gentlemen with years of practical site experience. They knew how things worked, why things worked and how to make things happen in the context of the way building sites work. They'd been there, done that and had got the fucking T-shirt.

On a practical level, these engineers gave you the specification info according to dimensions. Things like: 'This doorway needs to be four foot wide'. Clear and simple stuff. The foreman and the builder would also be party to these dimensions, and any one of the three could flag up anything they felt was wrong. It was a system that kept mistakes to a minimum. On the other hand, today's engineers tend to be young lads and lasses, fresh out of university with all the required qualifications but with little practical experience, and often none at all.

What's more, the old dimensions-based system has changed to one based on co-ordinates. These days we get given a CAD (computer aided design) drawing of whatever, accompanied by some complicated bullshit numbers. These numbers are downloaded into a variety of engineers' contraptions that then do things like projecting lasers towards certain points to guide edges and corners.

It's very clever stuff, but it's completely unnecessary and prone to mistakes being made when the engineers, with their lack of experience, don't get the numbers right and fuck things up. And because we aren't taught to understand these co-ordinates, we can't flag up any problems before they happen.

And do these bright young career-driven things want to learn from their mistakes? Do they buggery. They don't want to be engineers forever. They're just marking time so they can climb the greasy pole and become project managers. Old-school engineers understand the ins and outs of things, but these kids don't put the effort into grasping those practicalities because they don't feel it's of any relevance to their future careers. Great for them, but it makes life bloody hard for those of us that care about the actual work on the tools.

I personally think that academically-minded people and theoretical approaches are incompatible with good, effective construction. These people run everything 'by the book', by the paperwork and according to 'the system'. It's like David Walliams used to say in *Little Britain*: "Computer says no!"

For example, finishing work early results in a bollocking, even if it saves people money and the job's been done properly. This is because graduates can put an itinerary and a plan in place, but if you show that they got their plan wrong by finishing the job ahead of schedule, you're showing them up.

That's why you often see so many people stood around on building sites doing cock all: jobs are stretched out to fill up the hours allotted to do it, so that certain boxes can be ticked on plans and paperwork. The level of waste and unnecessary expense this is causing, particularly on public sector works where the money is ultimately coming from the taxpayer, is absolutely fucking obscene.

These graduates also haven't grasped that the blokes on the tools are generally more intelligent and savvy than they're given credit for, and are certainly smarter than they used to be. In the old days, the workforce used to be given orders and paperwork and told to get on with it, because the bosses knew better and had the knowledge advantage. But now that the all-important RAMS (Risk Assessment and Method Statements) are written by people with no practical experience, that advantage has disappeared.

This means workers can use any and every regulation to their benefit, and are far more able to find loopholes to get out of doing work. This can go as far as looking at every individual reference or date on a RAMS - for example, sign-off dates on scaffolding - and then pull the site managers up on the slightest inconsistency or technicality. If a RAMS isn't bulletproof, then the blokes are perfectly entitled to turn straight back round, get back into the break room, and carry on finishing the *Sun* crossword.

Ultimately, there is no value placed on experience in the industry any more. It doesn't matter if you're a labourer sweeping up or the big boss general foreman: experience and capability are now irrelevant if you haven't got the right ticket or qualification.

As construction is a constantly evolving industry, it needs workers with the right mental skills and mindset to operate in whatever evolving and unpredictable environments and challenges might be thrown at them. But because of this extra emphasis on paperwork and qualifications, people who have the awareness and common-sense to be excellent builders but who aren't strong academically are being frozen out of the industry. And even worse, they're frozen out in favour of those that can pass a test and get the ticket, but are fucking liabilities in the real world of a building site.

I guess all this sounds like I'm pining for the old days of working shirtless, dodgy scaffolding, no hard hats and four-pint lunch breaks. Trust me, I'm not. But unfortunately, seeing as the industry today prioritises paperwork, certificates and theories over practicality, manual skills and good old hard work, I'm actually pretty glad that I'll be retiring soon.

Printed in Great Britain
by Amazon